Black Woman

A Dedication to Chiquita D. Felder-Stephenson

The Journey of a Strong Black Woman in Today's World

By

Melvin Prince Johnakin

Black Woman, A Dedication to Chiquita D. Felder Stephenson, The Journey of a Strong Back Woman in Today's World

Copyright 2024 by Melvin Prince Johnakin

All rights reserved. No part of this publication may be reproduced, distributed, or transmitted in any form or by any means, including photocopying, recording, or other electronic or mechanical methods, without the prior written permission of the publisher, except in the case of brief quotations embodied in critical reviews and certain other noncommercial uses permitted by copyright law.

Although the author and publisher have made every effort to ensure that the information in this book was correct at press time, the author and publisher do not assume and hereby disclaim any liability to any party for any loss, damage, or disruption caused by errors or omissions, whether such errors or omissions result from negligence, accident, or any other cause. Adherence to all applicable laws and regulations, including international, federal, state, and local governing professional licensing, business practices, advertising, and all other aspects of doing business in the US, Canada or any other jurisdiction is the sole responsibility of the reader and consumer.

Neither the author nor the publisher assumes any responsibility or liability whatsoever on behalf of the consumer or reader of this material. Any perceived slight of any individual or organization is purely unintentional.

The resources in this book are provided for informational purposes only and should not be used to replace the specialized training and professional judgment of a health care or mental health care professional. Neither the author nor the publisher can be held responsible for the use of the information provided within this book. Please always consult a trained professional before making any decision regarding treatment of yourself or other.

Dedication

I am dedicating this book to a special woman Chiquita D. Felder-Stephenson who has unwavering resilience towards life and what she stands for.

A Black Woman in today's world showing struggles, and triumphs of Black women. A narrative a profound exploration that transcends mere storytelling to become an anthem for resilience, identity, and empowerment. This book does not just seek to portray the experiences of Black women; it aims to illuminate their journeys with authenticity, depth, and a powerful voice that resonates across generations.

Forward

From the very first page, Johnakin invites us into a world rich with the complexities of Black womanhood. His prose is not only lyrical but also grounded in the harsh realities and vibrant cultures that shape the lives of the women he writes about. This work is a testament to the strength and beauty of Black women, who have often been sidelined in historical narratives and societal discourses. Johnakin's commitment to elevating their stories is both timely and necessary, particularly in a world that continues to grapple with issues of race, gender, and equality.

"Black Woman" reflects the multifaceted experiences that define Black womanhood. Johnakin deftly navigates themes of struggle and triumph, love and loss, identity and liberation. He captures the essence of what it means to be a Black woman in today's society, intertwining personal anecdotes with broader cultural commentary. Each chapter unfolds like a new layer of an intricate quilt, revealing the diverse patterns of life that Black women weave through their resilience and creativity.

The book resonates with a sense of urgency, reminding us that the stories of Black women are not merely historical accounts but living narratives that continue to evolve. Johnakin draws upon rich historical contexts, seamlessly integrating the legacies of those who came before with the aspirations of those who will follow. Through his words, we are reminded of the powerful figures who have paved the way—artists, activists, mothers, and sisters—each contributing to a legacy that is both rich and complex.

One of the remarkable aspects of "Black Woman" is its ability to evoke empathy and understanding. Johnakin writes with a sincerity that breaks down barriers, inviting readers from all walks of life to engage with the experiences and emotions of Black women. He does not shy away from addressing uncomfortable truths, instead confronting them head-on with compassion and insight. This courage to tackle difficult topics makes the book not only a celebration of Black womanhood but also a call to action for all of us to recognize and challenge the systemic injustices that persist in our society.

Moreover, the narrative is punctuated by moments of joy and celebration. Johnakin masterfully highlights the resilience and creativity that define Black women, showcasing their contributions to art, culture, and society. He paints vivid portraits of women who have turned pain into power, using their experiences to inspire and uplift others. This balance between struggle and celebration is essential, as it encapsulates the reality of Black womanhood—one that is often overlooked in mainstream narratives.

As we delve deeper into "Black Woman," we are also prompted to reflect on our own roles within these narratives. Johnakin encourages readers to recognize the interconnectedness of our stories, urging us to listen, learn, and uplift those whose voices have been marginalized. This book serves as a reminder that understanding and empathy are not passive acts; they require active engagement and a willingness to confront our own biases and privileges.

Johnakin's work is not just for Black women; it is for anyone who seeks to understand the complexities of race and gender in contemporary society. It invites dialogue and reflection, fostering a deeper appreciation for the diverse experiences that shape our world. In an era where representation matters more than ever, "Black Woman" stands as a powerful testament to the strength and resilience of Black women, illuminating their stories in a way that is both poignant and impactful.

In conclusion, "Black Woman" is more than a book; it is a movement. Melvin Prince Johnakin has crafted a narrative that honors the past, speaks to the present, and inspires the future. His words affirm the beauty, strength, and complexity of Black womanhood, making this book an essential read for anyone seeking to understand the richness of these experiences. As you turn the pages, prepare to be moved, challenged, and inspired. Johnakin invites you to walk alongside him in this journey, to celebrate, to empathize, and to engage with the powerful stories of Black women.

Let us embrace this opportunity to listen, learn, and uplift. "Black Woman" is not just a collection of stories; it is a call to arms, a reminder that the narratives of Black women are integral to the fabric of our shared humanity. Together, let us honor these voices and ensure that they are never silenced again.

Chapter 1

Child of God

Being a child of God is a profound identity that transcends cultural, racial, and social boundaries. For Black women, this identity is a source of strength, hope, and resilience amidst the challenges of a world that often marginalizes their existence. In this chapter, we will explore the intersection of faith and identity, the unique experiences of Black women as children of God, and how this faith shapes their lives, relationships, and aspirations.

Embracing Identity

From the moment we come into this world, our identities are shaped by myriad factors: our families, communities, and the larger society. For many Black women, identity is intricately tied to both heritage and faith. Growing up in a community that celebrates the rich cultural tapestry of African American history, I learned early on about the significance of resilience. Our ancestors endured unimaginable hardships, yet their faith remained unshaken. This legacy serves as a constant reminder that our identity as children of God is both a privilege and a responsibility.

In many Black churches, the concept of being a child of God is celebrated with fervor. The church serves as a sanctuary, a place where the struggles of daily life fade in the presence of collective worship and praise. Here, we are not just members of a congregation; we are sisters, daughters, and warriors in faith. The stories of women like Sojourner Truth and Harriet Tubman resonate deeply, reminding us that faith can be a catalyst for change, courage, and liberation.

The Power of Faith

Faith is a powerful force, especially in a world that can be hostile to Black women. It offers solace in times of distress and a sense of belonging in a society that often feels isolated. As a child of God, I have found that faith provides a framework through which I can interpret my experiences, both joyous and painful.

In moments of doubt or despair, I reflect on the scripture from Isaiah 41:10: "Fear not, for I am with you; be not dismayed, for I am your God; I will strengthen you, I will help you, I will uphold you with my righteous right hand." This verse has been a lifeline, reminding me that I am never alone. It encourages me to lean into my faith, especially when faced with challenges that might seek to undermine my spirit.

The church has also been a crucial source of support, offering a community of women who uplift one another. In group prayers, Bible studies, and service projects, I have witnessed the transformative power of faith in action. Women gather to share their burdens, celebrate their victories, and pray for one another, creating an unbreakable bond that transcends individual struggles.

Navigating Societal Challenges

The world outside the church doors can be daunting. As a Black woman, I navigate a reality marked by systemic racism, gender inequality, and societal expectations. These challenges can sometimes feel overwhelming, but my faith serves as both a shield and a sword. It reminds me of my worth and the divine purpose that drives me forward.

For many Black women, the dual pressures of race and gender create a unique set of challenges in professional and personal environments. The workplace can often be fraught with microaggressions and stereotypes, but my faith encourages me to stand firm. I draw strength from the knowledge that I am created in the image of God, deserving of respect and dignity.

When faced with adversity, I find comfort in the biblical story of Esther. Her journey from an orphan to a queen illustrates not only the importance of courage but also the significance of divine timing. Esther's faith and bravery in the face of danger remind me that my own struggles are part of a larger narrative. I am called to be a voice for the voiceless and to advocate for justice, not only for myself but for others who may feel marginalized.

The Role of Community

Community is integral to the life of a child of God. In my experience, the Black church has been a cornerstone of support, providing a space where faith and culture intertwine. It is here that I have witnessed the Incredible resilience of Black women, who often take on roles as leaders, nurturers, and advocates within their communities.

The collective strength of Black women is palpable in church gatherings, where we share our stories of triumph and struggle. These moments of vulnerability build a tapestry of shared experiences that foster deeper connections. We learn from one another, drawing inspiration from the diverse journeys represented in our pews.

Moreover, the church often serves as a hub for social justice initiatives, providing a platform for us to address issues impacting our communities. Through outreach programs, advocacy, and education, we extend our faith beyond the walls of the church, embodying the teachings of Christ in our actions. This commitment to service reinforces our identity as children of God, reminding us that our faith is not just a personal journey but a communal responsibility.

Spiritual Growth and Self-Care

Being a child of God also requires intentionality in nurturing one's spiritual life. For Black women, this can sometimes be a juggling act, balancing the demands of work, family, and personal aspirations. However, prioritizing spiritual growth is essential for maintaining mental and emotional well-being.

Prayer, meditation, and scripture study are vital components of my spiritual practice. They provide moments of reflection and clarity, allowing me to reconnect with my purpose and divine identity. In a world that often tries to define me by external factors, these practices remind me of who I am in Christ—a beloved child with inherent worth and purpose.

Self-care is another crucial aspect of this journey. It is easy to get caught up in the hustle of life and neglect our own needs. However, I have learned that taking time to recharge is not only beneficial but necessary. Engaging in activities that bring joy—be it art, music, or simply spending time in nature—nourishes my spirit and allows me to approach life with renewed energy and perspective.

Faith as a Catalyst for Change

As Black women, our faith often compels us to act, to fight for justice and equality. This activism is rooted in the biblical call to love our neighbors and seek justice. The story of the Good Samaritan resonates deeply, challenging us to look beyond our circumstances and extend compassion to those in need.

Many Black women have historically played critical roles in movements for civil rights and social change. Figures like Fannie Lou Hamer and Angela Davis remind us that activism is an expression of our faith, a manifestation of our commitment to justice. In today's world, we continue this legacy, using our voices and platforms to advocate for change.

Social media has become a powerful tool for this advocacy, allowing us to raise awareness about issues affecting our communities. Through hashtags, campaigns, and online discussions, we amplify our voices and connect with others committed to the same cause. Our faith encourages us to speak truth to power, reminding us that we are agents of change, called to be the light in a world that can often feel dark.

Conclusion: A Legacy of Faith

As I reflect on my journey as a Black woman and a child of God, I am filled with gratitude for the strength that faith provides. It is a guiding light that illuminates my path, offering hope in times of uncertainty and joy in moments of celebration. My identity as a child of God shapes not only how I see myself but also how I engage with the world around me.

In a society that often seeks to diminish our worth, we must remember our divine heritage and the power that comes from being children of God. We are resilient, capable, and deserving of love and respect. As we embrace this identity, we not only empower ourselves but also uplift those around us, creating a legacy of faith, strength, and unwavering hope.

In the words of Maya Angelou, "I can be changed by what happens to me. But I refuse to be reduced by it." As Black women, we are multifaceted beings, shaped by our experiences yet defined by our faith. Our stories are powerful, our voices are needed, and our legacy is one of unbreakable strength. Together, we will continue to rise, embodying the love and grace of being children of God in a world that desperately needs our light.

Chapter 2

Fighting Cancer

Cancer is a word that can evoke fear, uncertainty, and a myriad of emotions. For many Black women, the battle against cancer is not just a personal struggle; it is a journey that intersects with issues of race, gender, health disparities, and systemic inequalities. This chapter explores the unique challenges faced by Black women diagnosed with cancer, the resilience they embody, and the community support that plays a vital role in their fight. Through personal narratives, medical insights, and reflections on spirituality, we will navigate the complexities of this journey together.

Understanding the Landscape

The statistics surrounding cancer in the Black community are sobering. According to the American Cancer Society, Black women are more likely to be diagnosed with aggressive forms of breast cancer and face higher mortality rates compared to their white counterparts. This disparity can be attributed to a combination of factors, including socioeconomic status, access to healthcare, and systemic racism within the medical system. Understanding these factors is crucial for addressing the broader context of cancer care for Black women.

Many Black women may encounter barriers when seeking medical attention. These barriers can include mistrust of the healthcare system, often rooted in historical injustices, as well as financial constraints that limit access to quality care. The fear of being dismissed or not taken seriously can lead to delays in diagnosis and treatment, exacerbating health outcomes. Addressing these systemic issues is crucial in creating a more equitable healthcare environment.

Personal Narratives: A Journey Begins

Every cancer journey is unique, shaped by individual experiences, fears, and hopes. For me, the journey began with a routine check-up that revealed a lump in my breast. At first, I dismissed it as nothing more than a fibroid or a benign cyst. However, the nagging feeling that something was wrong prompted me to seek a second opinion. This decision would change my life forever.

When I received the diagnosis of breast cancer, a whirlwind of emotions swept over me: shock, fear, and an overwhelming sense of vulnerability. I remember sitting in the doctor's office, staring at the ground, trying to process the words that echoed in my mind. The reality of cancer felt foreign, yet it was now a part of my identity. In that moment, I realized that I had to fight—not just for myself but for my family, my community, and all the women who came before me.

The Role of Community

One of the most powerful aspects of fighting cancer as a Black woman is the sense of community that often emerges. Family, friends, and support networks play an invaluable role in this journey. As I navigated my treatment, I found solace in the love and support of those around me. They became my warriors, attending appointments with me, helping me keep track of medications, and providing meals during the days when I was too exhausted to cook.

Support groups specifically for Black women facing cancer can also provide a safe space for sharing experiences and resources. These groups foster a sense of belonging and understanding, where members can relate to each other's struggles and triumphs. The power of shared stories cannot be underestimated; they remind us that we are not alone in this fight. Hearing the stories of other Women, some who had fought and triumphed, gave me hope and strength to continue my own battle.

Navigating Treatment

The journey through cancer treatment can be overwhelming, particularly when faced with the complexities of the medical system. I underwent a series of tests, surgeries, and treatments, each accompanied by its own set of challenges. From chemotherapy to radiation, the physical and emotional toll was significant. It was during these times that my faith and resilience were truly tested.

One of the most challenging aspects of treatment was managing the side effects. Chemotherapy left me fatigued, nauseous, and emotionally drained. I often found comfort in my faith, turning to prayer and meditation to find peace amidst the chaos. I also sought out holistic practices, such as yoga and mindfulness, which helped me connect with my body and manage stress.

As a Black woman, I was acutely aware of the importance of advocating for myself within the healthcare system. I learned to ask questions, seek second opinions, and demand thorough explanations of my treatment plan. This advocacy was not just about my own health but about breaking down barriers for others who might feel intimidated or marginalized in medical environments. I realized that my voice mattered, and I was determined to use it.

The Intersection of Race and Health

The intersection of race and health is a crucial aspect of the cancer journey for Black women. Studies have shown that implicit biases can influence the quality of care received by patients of color. For example, many Black women report feeling dismissed or not taken seriously by healthcare providers. This reality can lead to delayed diagnoses and inadequate treatment options.

Throughout my journey, I encountered moments where I felt the weight of these biases. There were instances when I sensed that my concerns were minimized or overlooked. It was a painful reminder that the fight against cancer was not just a personal battle; it was also a struggle against systemic inequities. This awareness fueled my determination to advocate not only for myself but for other Black women who might face similar challenges.

Finding Strength in Faith

For many Black women, faith is a source of strength during difficult times. In the face of cancer, I found comfort in scripture and prayer. Verses like Psalm 30:5, which reminds us that "weeping may endure for a night, but joy comes in the morning," became anchors during my darkest days. The promise of hope and healing resonated deeply within me.

Faith also played a role in fostering resilience. I learned to lean into my spiritual community for support, finding solace in prayer circles and gatherings that uplifted my spirit. Sharing my struggles with others who understood the importance of faith provided a sense of connection and purpose. We prayed for healing, strength, and peace, reminding each other that we were not alone in our battles.

The Importance of Education and Awareness

Raising awareness about cancer within the Black community is crucial for early detection and prevention. Education about risk factors, symptoms, and the importance of regular screenings can empower women to take control of their health. As I progressed through my treatment, I made it a priority to share my story and educate others about the realities of cancer.

Community outreach programs focused on health education can play a transformative role. Engaging with local organizations to provide resources and information about cancer screenings, healthy lifestyles, and support services helps dismantle barriers to care. By sharing my experiences and knowledge, I hope to inspire other women to prioritize their health and advocate for themselves.

Celebrating Resilience

As I reflect on my journey, I am struck by the incredible resilience of Black women facing cancer. Each story is a testament to strength, courage, and the unwavering spirit that defines our community. Celebrating these stories is essential, not just for individual healing but for collective empowerment.

I remember attending a cancer survivors' event where women shared their journeys, laughter, and tears filling the room. It was a celebration of resilience, a reminder that we are more than our diagnoses. We are warriors, advocates, and survivors, each with a unique story that deserves to be heard.

These events also serve as platforms for raising awareness about the unique challenges faced by Black women in their cancer journeys. By coming together, we amplify our voices and create a movement that seeks to address health disparities and advocate for systemic change.

Moving Forward: Advocacy and Empowerment

The fight against cancer does not end with treatment; it evolves into a lifelong journey of advocacy and empowerment. As a survivor, I am committed to using my voice to advocate for better healthcare access and education within the Black community. I believe that by sharing our stories, we can inspire change and support one another in our journeys.

Engaging in advocacy work can take many forms, from participating in awareness campaigns to speaking at community events. It is essential to create spaces where Black women can share their experiences, access resources, and find support. By fostering a culture of empowerment, we can challenge the systemic barriers that persist in healthcare.

Conclusion: A Legacy of Strength

Fighting cancer as a Black woman in today's world is a journey filled with challenges, but it is also a testament to the strength, resilience, and unity of our community. Each diagnosis is not just an individual battle; it is a call to action for collective empowerment and advocacy.

As I continue my journey, I am reminded of the words of Maya Angelou: "I can be changed by what happens to me. But I refuse to be reduced by it." My experience with cancer has changed me, but it has also ignited a fire within me to fight for myself and others. Together, we can create a legacy of strength, resilience, and hope for future generations of Black women.

In the face of adversity, we rise. In the shadow of cancer, we shine. Our stories matter, our voices need to be heard, and our fight is far from over. We are warriors, and together, we will continue to break barriers, inspire change, and uplift each other in this journey of life.

Chapter 3

High Level Politics

The world of high-level politics can often seem impenetrable, a realm dominated by powerful figures whose decisions shape the lives of millions. For a Black woman, entering and thriving in this arena presents unique challenges and opportunities. Throughout history, women of color have faced systemic barriers, yet they have also carved out spaces for themselves, proving that resilience, intellect, and determination can change the narrative. This chapter explores the complexities of navigating high-level politics as a Black woman, highlighting personal experiences, the intersections of race and gender, and the power of community and advocacy.

My journey into politics began not with a grand vision of power but with a desire to effect change in my community. Growing up in a neighborhood marked by socioeconomic challenges, I witnessed firsthand the impact of political decisions on everyday lives. Education, healthcare, housing, and employment were not just abstract policies; they were the fabric of my community's existence. It was this understanding that ignited my passion for public service.

In college, I majored in political science, immersing myself in the history of civil rights and social justice movements. I was inspired by trailblazers like Shirley Chisholm, who became the first Black woman elected to the United States Congress, and Kamala Harris, the first Black woman to serve as Vice President. Their stories fueled my ambition and made me believe that I could also make a difference. However, I quickly learned that the path I chose was fraught with challenges, particularly as a Black woman in a predominantly white, male-dominated field.

The intersection of race and gender plays a significant role in the experiences of Black women in politics. As I entered the political arena, I was acutely aware of the dual biases I would face. While my qualifications were strong, I often found myself battling stereotypes that questioned my competence and legitimacy. The imposter syndrome was a constant companion, whispering doubts in my ear, but I refused to let it define me.

In meetings and negotiations, I often felt the weight of scrutiny more heavily than my colleagues. A shared glance or a dismissive comment could cut deep, reminding me that I was not just representing myself, but also my community and all Black women striving for recognition in this space. It became essential to cultivate a strong sense of self-worth, to remind myself that my voice mattered and that I belonged in these discussions.

Navigating high-level politics requires not just individual strength but also the ability to build alliances and networks. Early in my career, I understood the importance of connection. I sought mentorship from seasoned politicians and community leaders who could guide me through the complexities of the political landscape. These mentors became invaluable resources, offering insights and encouragement that helped me establish my footing.

One of the most impactful moments came during a policy summit aimed at addressing disparities in healthcare access. I met a group of women who shared similar experiences and aspirations. We bonded over our struggles and triumphs, forming a network of support that would prove crucial as we navigated our political careers. This sisterhood became a source of strength, reminding us that we were not alone in our journeys.

As I climbed the political ladder, I made it a priority to uplift other women of color. I organized workshops and networking events, creating spaces where we could share knowledge and resources. By fostering an environment of collaboration, we not only expanded our influence but also challenged the status quo that often pits women against each other in competitive environments.

Representation is a powerful force in politics. As a Black woman in a high-level position, I recognized the responsibility that came with my role. I understood that my presence was not just about personal achievement; it was about paving the way for future generations. When young girls of color saw me in positions of power, I hoped they would see possibilities for themselves.

During a press conference addressing a critical policy initiative aimed at improving education in underserved communities, I shared my personal story of growing up in a similar environment. The response was overwhelming. Young girls reached out to me through social media, expressing their dreams of entering politics and making a difference. It was a powerful reminder that representation matters; it inspires hope and ignites ambition.

However, representation also comes with scrutiny. I often found myself in the spotlight, where my every word and action were analyzed. It was crucial to remain authentic while navigating this pressure. I learned to embrace my identity and use my experiences as a lens through which to view policy decisions, ensuring that they were inclusive and equitable.

Advocating for policy change as a Black woman in politics is a multifaceted endeavor. The complexities of legislation often mean that progress is slow and filled with obstacles. I encountered resistance from colleagues who were reluctant to address issues that disproportionately affected marginalized communities. This resistance was often rooted in a lack of understanding or empathy—a barrier I was determined to dismantle.

One significant challenge arose during discussions about healthcare reform. As we debated the merits of various proposals, I pushed for measures that would specifically address the disparities faced by Black women in accessing care. I presented data showing how systemic inequities impacted health outcomes, but the conversation often turned into a numbers game, overshadowing the human aspect of the issue.

In these moments, I learned the importance of storytelling. Sharing personal narratives and those of constituents affected by these policies helped humanize the statistics. I organized town halls, bringing community members into the conversation to share their lived experiences. This approach shifted the dialogue, compelling my colleagues to reconsider their positions and understand the urgency of our advocacy.

The path through high-level politics is not without its battles. There were moments when I felt overwhelmed by the weight of expectations and the challenges of navigating a system that often seemed resistant to change. In these times, resilience became my guiding principle.

I recall a particularly challenging campaign season when I faced intense scrutiny from both opponents and the media. Mischaracterizations and unfounded rumors circulated, threatening to undermine my credibility. Instead of succumbing to despair, I leaned into my support network, seeking solace and strength from friends, family, and mentors. Their encouragement reminded me of my purpose and the impact I aimed to achieve.

Resilience also meant maintaining a sense of humor and perspective. I learned to celebrate small victories and acknowledge the efforts of my team, understanding that each step forward was a part of a larger journey. This mindset not only bolstered my spirit but also fostered a positive atmosphere within my team, allowing us to tackle challenges collaboratively.

In the high-stakes world of politics, self-care and spirituality became essential components of my journey. The demands of the job often left little room for rest, but I knew that to be an effective leader, I had to prioritize my well-being. I turned to meditation, prayer, and mindfulness practices to ground myself amidst the chaos.

Spirituality provided a framework for understanding my purpose and the impact I wanted to make. It reminded me that my work was not just about political power but about serving my community and uplifting others. This perspective helped me navigate the inevitable challenges with grace and determination.

I also made it a priority to advocate for self-care among my colleagues. I organized wellness workshops and encouraged open conversations about mental health within our political circles. By fostering a culture that valued well-being, we could better support one another and tackle the challenges we faced in our work.

As I reflect on my journey in high-level politics, I am acutely aware of the legacy I hope to leave behind. It is not just about personal achievements but about creating pathways for others to follow. I envision a future where the halls of power are filled with diverse voices, each contributing to a richer, more equitable political landscape.

To build this legacy, I have committed to mentoring young women of color who aspire to enter politics. By sharing my experiences and insights, I aim to empower the next generation of leaders. I encourage them to embrace their unique perspectives and advocate for the issues that matter most to their communities.

Moreover, I have sought to engage in broader advocacy efforts that address systemic inequalities. Collaborating with organizations focused on social justice, education, and healthcare reform allows me to amplify our collective voices and drive meaningful change.

Navigating the highest levels of politics as a Black woman is a journey marked by challenges, triumphs, and an unwavering commitment to justice and equity. It is a path that demands resilience, courage, and a deep understanding of the complexities of race and gender.

As I continue to forge my way through the political landscape, I am reminded of the importance of community and collaboration. Together, we can create a future where diverse voices are not only heard but celebrated. We can dismantle the barriers that have long hindered progress and create a political environment that reflects the richness of our society.

In the words of Audre Lorde, "I am not free while any woman is unfree, even when her shackles are very different from my own." This sentiment resonates deeply as I navigate my journey. My fight for justice is intertwined with the struggles of others, and together, we will rise.

As we look to the future, let us remember that our power lies in our unity. By supporting one another, sharing our stories, and advocating for change, we can create a legacy of empowerment that transcends generations. The halls of power are changing, and as Black women, we will continue to assert our place within them, not just as participants but as leaders shaping a brighter future for all.

Chapter 4

Loving My Support System: The Bond with My Daughter as a Black Woman

Being a Black woman in today's world comes with its unique set of challenges and triumphs. As I navigate the complexities of life—career, relationships, and personal growth—one of my most profound sources of strength and joy is my daughter. Our bond transcends the typical mother-daughter relationship; it is a partnership rooted in love, resilience, and mutual support. This chapter explores the transformative power of our relationship, the importance of nurturing a supportive environment, and the lessons learned as we journey through life together.

Motherhood is a gift that reshapes one's identity. From the moment I held my daughter in my arms, I was filled with a love so profound it took my breath away. She became my motivation, my reason to strive for better, and my inspiration to navigate the complexities of life with grace and determination. As a Black woman, I am acutely aware of the responsibilities that come with motherhood—especially in a society that often marginalizes our experiences and voices.

Raising a daughter in a world that can be unforgiving requires intentionality and strength. I strive to create a nurturing environment where she feels safe, loved, and empowered to express herself. This commitment to motherhood has deepened my understanding of love, resilience, and the importance of support systems. Together, we navigate the intricacies of our identities, celebrating our heritage and fostering a sense of belonging.

At the heart of our relationship is a strong foundation built on trust and open communication. From a young age, I encouraged my daughter to share her feelings, thoughts, and dreams. We created a space where she could express herself without fear of judgment—a sanctuary where her voice matters. This practice not only strengthens our bond but also empowers her to be confident in her identity.

I remember a particularly poignant moment when she was in elementary school. One day, she came home upset after a classmate made a hurtful comment about her hair. I could see the pain in her eyes, and it broke my heart. Instead of dismissing her feelings, I sat down with her, listened intently, and encouraged her to express how she felt. We talked about the beauty of her curls and the history behind them—the rich legacy of our ancestors who wore their hair with pride. This conversation not only validated her feelings but also instilled a sense of pride in her identity.

Through these moments, I have learned that nurturing a supportive environment is essential for her emotional growth. By fostering open dialogue, I help her navigate the complexities of being a Black girl in a world that often imposes rigid standards of beauty and behavior. Our conversations are not just about addressing challenges; they are also celebrations of our culture, our achievements, and our dreams.

As I reflect on my journey as a mother, I recognize the importance of love and support in shaping my daughter's self-esteem and resilience. My love for her is unconditional, a steady force that anchors her amidst life's storms. I strive to be her biggest cheerleader, celebrating her achievements and encouraging her to pursue her passions wholeheartedly.

One of the most significant ways I show my support is by actively participating in her interests. Whether it's attending her dance recitals, helping with school projects, or engaging in her hobbies, I make it a priority to be present. These moments not only strengthen our bond but also demonstrate to her that her passions matter. My involvement sends a powerful message: she is valued, and her dreams are worth pursuing.

In our household, we also prioritize the importance of community. I encourage her to build relationships with other girls, creating a support system that extends beyond our family. We often host gatherings with friends, fostering an environment where laughter, creativity, and collaboration thrive. Witnessing her interact with peers, share ideas, and support one another fills me with immense pride. It is a reminder that love and support can come from many sources, creating a network of strength and encouragement.

Life is not without challenges, and as Black women, we often face unique adversities. The world can be harsh, and I want my daughter to be equipped with the tools to navigate it with resilience. We talk openly about the injustices that exist and the importance of standing up for oneself and others. I want her to understand that while she may encounter obstacles, she possesses the strength to overcome them.

One particularly challenging time was during the pandemic. We were all grappling with uncertainty, and I could see the impact on her emotional well-being. To combat feelings of isolation, we established a routine that included daily check-ins, creative projects, and virtual hangouts with friends. We also made a point to engage in community service, finding ways to give back and connect with our neighbors, even from a distance.

Through these experiences, I emphasized the importance of resilience. I shared stories of our ancestors—women who faced unimaginable challenges yet remained steadfast in their faith and determination. These narratives became a source of inspiration for both of us, reminding her that adversity can be a catalyst for growth.

In a world that often sends mixed messages about beauty and worth, I am committed to instilling a sense of self-love in my daughter. I want her to know that she is enough just as she is, and that her worth is not defined by societal standards. This journey of self-love is ongoing, and it requires intentionality and reinforcement.

We engage in activities that promote self-care and self-reflection. Whether it's journaling, practicing mindfulness, or simply taking a moment to appreciate her unique qualities, I encourage her to prioritize her well-being. I often remind her of the importance of affirmations—powerful statements that reinforce her worth and abilities.

Together, we create a list of affirmations that resonate with her, and we recite them regularly. This practice has become a cherished ritual, a way for her to embrace her identity and build confidence.

I also emphasize the importance of surrounding herself with positive influences. We discuss the qualities of true friendships and the value of uplifting one another. In a world that can sometimes feel competitive, I want her to thrive in relationships that foster support and encouragement. This commitment to self-love and positive connections lays the groundwork for her future relationships, helping her establish healthy boundaries and cultivate meaningful connections.

As a Black woman, embracing our heritage and culture is integral to our identity. I am passionate about teaching my daughter about our rich history, the contributions of Black women, and the beauty of our cultural traditions. I want her to understand the significance of our ancestry and the strength that comes from knowing where we came from.

We celebrate cultural milestones together—attending events like Black History Month programs, local festivals, and community gatherings. These experiences allow her to connect with our roots and foster a sense of pride in her identity. We often engage in discussions about historical figures who have paved the way for us, from Harriet Tubman to Michelle Obama. These conversations not only educate her about our past but also inspire her to envision her own future.

Additionally, we incorporate cultural practices into our daily lives. Whether it's cooking traditional dishes, listening to music that reflects our heritage, or participating in community events, these practices strengthen our connection to our culture. I want her to understand that our identity is not just about the struggles we face but also about the beauty, creativity, and resilience that define us.

While I strive to empower my daughter, I am also acutely aware of the societal challenges that come with being a Black woman. Conversations about race, identity, and social justice are essential, and I approach them with care and honesty. I want her to be aware of the realities of our world without feeling overwhelmed by fear.

We discuss current events, exploring issues related to racism, inequality, and injustice. I encourage her to think critically about these topics and to engage in conversations with her peers. It is essential for her to understand the importance of advocacy and activism. Together, we participate in community initiatives that promote social change, reinforcing the idea that we can be agents of change in our own right.

One impactful experience was attending a local march for racial justice. It was a moment of empowerment, witnessing individuals from diverse backgrounds come together to stand against injustice. I saw my daughter's eyes light up as she realized the strength of community and the collective power we hold when we unite for a common cause. This experience helped her to connect her personal identity to a larger movement, fostering a sense of responsibility and agency.

At the core of our relationship is a love that knows no bounds. It is a love that celebrates our individuality while embracing our shared experiences as Black women. I cherish the moments we spend together—whether it's cooking in the kitchen, laughing during movie nights, or having deep conversations about life. These moments create lasting memories and reinforce our bond.

I often remind my daughter that love is not just about words; it is about actions. I strive to show her love in tangible ways, whether through small gestures like leaving notes of encouragement or planning special outings together. I want her to feel cherished, to know that she is deserving of love and joy in every aspect of her life.

Moreover, I emphasize the importance of selflessness and compassion. We engage in acts of kindness together, whether it's volunteering at local shelters or supporting community initiatives. These experiences teach her the value of empathy and the impact of giving back, reinforcing the idea that love extends beyond our immediate circle.

As I look to the future, I am filled with hope and excitement for what lies ahead for both of us. I envision a world where my daughter can thrive as her authentic self, unencumbered by societal limitations. I am committed to providing her with the tools and support she needs to navigate life's challenges and embrace her dreams.

I encourage her to pursue her passions fearlessly, whether in academics, the arts, or social activism. I want her to understand that her potential is limitless and that she has the power to shape her own destiny. My role is to be her guide, her confidante, and her unwavering supporter as she navigates the path ahead.

The bond I share with my daughter as a Black woman is a testament to the power of love, resilience, and community. Together, we navigate the complexities of life, drawing strength from our shared experiences and heritage. Our journey is not just a reflection of our individual identities; it is a celebration of the beauty and strength of Black womanhood.

As we continue to grow together, I am committed to nurturing our relationship and fostering an environment where she feels empowered to embrace her identity. Our love is a source of strength, a reminder that we are not alone in our journey. Together, we will face the challenges ahead, celebrate our victories, and create a legacy of love and resilience that will endure for generations to come. In her, I see the promise of a brighter future, and I am honored to be her mother and her support system.

Chapter 5

The Power of Being a Brand as a Black Woman

In a world where identity is often commodified, the notion of being a brand transcends mere marketing; it becomes a powerful narrative of self-representation and cultural significance. For Black women, the journey of branding is intricately tied to history, resilience, and the celebration of multifaceted identities. This chapter explores the nuances of being a brand as a Black woman, emphasizing the importance of authenticity, community, and empowerment.

Branding is fundamentally about identity. For Black women, identity is woven with layers of cultural heritage, personal experiences, and societal perceptions. Each woman carries a unique story, influenced by her background, upbringing, and the socio-political landscape. Recognizing these intersections is crucial in crafting a brand that is not only personal but also resonates with a broader audience.

The history of Black women is rich and complex. From the strength of ancestral legacies to the struggles against systemic oppression, Black women have always been at the forefront of social change. This historical context shapes how they approach branding. Their narratives are often rooted in resilience, community, and the fight for equity. When Black women build brands, they are not just selling a product or service; they are telling their stories and those of their ancestors.

Authenticity is the cornerstone of any successful brand. For Black women, authenticity means embracing their true selves, celebrating their unique experiences, and showcasing their cultural heritage. It involves rejecting stereotypes and societal expectations, allowing their individuality to shine. This authenticity resonates with audiences, fostering genuine connections and loyalty.

Storytelling is an essential aspect of branding. Black women have powerful stories that reflect their journeys, struggles, and triumphs. By sharing their narratives, they can create a brand that is relatable and inspiring. Whether through social media, blogs, or public speaking, storytelling allows Black women to connect with their audience on a personal level, building trust and engagement.

A brand's visual identity plays a significant role in how it is perceived. For Black women, incorporating elements of their culture—such as colors, patterns, and symbols—can create a strong visual representation of their brand. This not only celebrates their heritage but also challenges the often-Eurocentric standards of beauty and aesthetics in branding.

Community is vital in the journey of branding. For Black women, creating and nurturing a supportive network can amplify their voices and reach. Collaborating with other Black women entrepreneurs and creatives fosters a sense of solidarity and shared purpose. This community can serve as a source of inspiration, mentorship, and resources, making the branding journey less isolating.

In the competitive landscape of entrepreneurship, collaboration can be a powerful tool. Black women can uplift each other by sharing knowledge, resources, and platforms. This collaborative spirit not only strengthens individual brands but also enriches the collective narrative of Black womanhood. Collaborations can take many forms, from joint ventures to co-hosted events, amplifying each brand's visibility and impact.

Black women often confront stereotypes and biases that can hinder their branding efforts. The intersection of race and gender creates unique challenges, from microaggressions to outright discrimination. Navigating these obstacles requires resilience and strategic thinking. By acknowledging these challenges, Black women can develop strategies to counteract negative perceptions and assert their authority in their respective fields.

Social media offers a powerful platform for Black women to challenge stereotypes and redefine narratives. By curating their online presence, they can share their stories, showcase their work, and connect with like-minded individuals. Social media also provides an opportunity to engage directly with their audience, fostering a sense of community and belonging.

As Black women build their brands, they can also advocate for representation and inclusivity within their industries. By using their platforms to highlight issues of social justice, they not only elevate their brands but also contribute to a larger movement for change. This advocacy can take many forms—supporting other Black-owned businesses, engaging in community initiatives, or using their voice to raise awareness about important issues.

Building a brand offers Black women the opportunity for financial independence. By creating their own businesses, they can define their paths and break free from traditional employment constraints. This financial autonomy not only empowers them personally but also allows them to invest in their communities and support other Black women entrepreneurs.

Branding is not just about the present; it's about creating a legacy for future generations. By establishing successful brands, Black women can pave the way for young girls who aspire to follow in their footsteps. This legacy is about more than just business success; it's about instilling values of resilience, creativity, and empowerment in the next generation.

As Black women succeed in their branding endeavors, they become role models for others. Their journeys can inspire young Black girls to embrace their individuality, pursue their passions, and challenge societal norms. This ripple effect of empowerment is a testament to the power of branding as a tool for social change.

Being a brand as a Black woman is a profound journey of self-discovery, empowerment, and community building. It is about embracing authenticity, navigating challenges, and celebrating the richness of one's identity. In a society that often marginalizes Black voices, the act of branding becomes a powerful declaration of existence and significance. As Black women continue to carve out their spaces in the world, they not only uplift themselves but also inspire future generations to do the same. Through their brands, they tell their stories, challenge the status quo, and create a legacy of empowerment that will endure for years to come.

Chapter 6

The Art of Running a Household as a Black Mother in Today's World

In the tapestry of modern life, the role of a mother is both timeless and ever evolving. For Black mothers, this role encompasses a unique blend of cultural heritage, resilience, and the realities of navigating a world that often presents systemic challenges. Running a household as a Black mother today is not merely about managing daily tasks; it is about fostering a nurturing environment, instilling values, advocating for one's family, and celebrating identity amidst adversity. This chapter delves into the multifaceted experience of Black motherhood, highlighting the strengths, challenges, and triumphs that define this journey.

At the heart of running a household as a Black mother is the rich tapestry of cultural heritage and identity. Black motherhood is steeped in traditions that celebrate resilience, community, and love. From storytelling to cooking soul food, these practices are not just rituals; they are essential threads that weave the family's identity. By instilling these values in their children, Black mothers create a strong sense of belonging and pride.

A household should be a sanctuary, offering safety and comfort. Black mothers often go to great lengths to create an environment where their children feel secure, loved, and valued. This involves not only physical safety but also emotional well-being. Open communication, active listening, and unconditional support are vital components of fostering a nurturing home. Black mothers teach their children to express themselves and embrace their emotions, laying the groundwork for healthy relationships and self-esteem.

In today's world, Black mothers frequently juggle multiple responsibilities—caregiver, breadwinner, educator, and advocate. This multitasking can be overwhelming, yet Black mothers often find strength in their ability to adapt and persevere. The balancing act requires efficient time management, prioritization, and the ability to seek help when needed. Establishing routines helps maintain order and predictability, allowing families to navigate the complexities of daily life.

Amidst the demands of running a household, self-care is crucial yet often overlooked. Black mothers must prioritize their own well-being to care for their families effectively. This can include carving out time for relaxation, pursuing hobbies, and maintaining social connections. By modeling self-care, mothers teach their children the importance of mental health and personal wellness. Even small rituals, like enjoying a warm cup of tea or taking a quiet moment, can rejuvenate the spirit.

Education is a cornerstone of opportunity, and Black mothers play a pivotal role in advocating for their children's educational needs. This advocacy often involves navigating complex school systems, ensuring that their children receive equitable resources, and challenging bias when necessary. Black mothers are fierce protectors of their children's right to a quality education, often becoming involved in school boards, parent-teacher associations, and community organizations.

Beyond advocacy, Black mothers instill a love for learning in their children. This can be achieved through engaging activities, such as reading together, exploring cultural history, and encouraging curiosity. By creating a home environment rich in educational resources—books, art supplies, and technology—mothers empower their children to pursue knowledge passionately. Celebrating academic achievements, no matter how small, reinforces the value of education and hard work.

Black mothers often face systemic barriers that complicate their roles. From economic disparities to racial bias in healthcare and education, these challenges can be daunting. However, resilience is a hallmark of Black motherhood. Many mothers find creative solutions to overcome obstacles, whether through community support, resourcefulness, or advocacy. Building connections with other mothers can provide a support network that alleviates stress and fosters collaboration in addressing these challenges.

Mental health is a critical aspect of running a household, yet it is often stigmatized within communities. Black mothers are increasingly recognizing the importance of mental health and seeking support for themselves and their families. Open conversations about mental health help destigmatize the topic, allowing children to understand and manage their emotions healthily. By prioritizing mental wellness, Black mothers equip their children with tools to navigate life's challenges.

Community is an essential pillar in the lives of Black mothers. It provides a network of support, shared resources, and a sense of belonging. Many Black mothers actively engage with their communities, forming bonds with other families who share similar values and experiences. This communal spirit allows for collective childcare, shared knowledge, and emotional support, creating a safety net that enriches family life.

Black mothers often take the lead in celebrating cultural heritage within their households. This includes participating in traditions, holidays, and community events that resonate with their identity. By celebrating Black culture, mothers instill a sense of pride in their children, teaching them about their roots and the contributions of their ancestors. These celebrations reinforce the importance of cultural identity, fostering resilience and self-worth.

Financial literacy is a crucial skill that Black mothers strive to impart to their children. By teaching budgeting, saving, and investing, mothers empower their children to make informed financial decisions. This knowledge is particularly vital in a world where economic disparities persist. Black mothers often emphasize the importance of education as a pathway to financial independence, encouraging their children to pursue careers that align with their passions and strengths.

In today's society, understanding social justice is vital. Black mothers educate their children about equity, advocacy, and the importance of standing up against injustice. By discussing current events and historical struggles, they prepare their children to be informed citizens who actively participate in shaping a more equitable world. This education fosters empathy, critical thinking, and a commitment to social responsibility.

Running a household as a Black mother in today's world is a profound journey filled with challenges and triumphs. It is an art that requires resilience, creativity, and unwavering love. By nurturing their families, advocating for education, and celebrating cultural heritage, Black mothers not only create a safe and empowering home environment but also pave the way for future generations. Their strength and determination serve as a testament to the power of motherhood, illustrating that even amidst adversity, love and community can flourish. In this tapestry of Black motherhood, each thread tells a story of resilience, identity, and hope—creating a legacy that will endure for years to come.

Chapter 7

Empowering Entrepreneurship: Running a Business as a Black Woman

In today's dynamic economic landscape, Black women are emerging as formidable entrepreneurs, carving out spaces that reflect their unique experiences, perspectives, and aspirations. Running a business as a Black woman is not just about financial independence; it is a powerful act of self-determination, resilience, and community upliftment. This chapter explores the multifaceted journey of Black women entrepreneurs, highlighting the challenges they face, the strategies they employ, and the profound impact they have on their communities and industries.

The rise of Black woman entrepreneurship is a significant movement that has gained momentum over the past few years. According to research from the National Association of Women Business Owners, Black women are starting businesses at a faster rate than any other demographic group in the United States. This surge is a response to both a desire for economic empowerment and a need to address the systemic barriers that have historically limited their opportunities.

At the core of this movement is an entrepreneurial spirit characterized by innovation, resilience, and community orientation. Black women entrepreneurs often draw from their personal experiences and cultural heritage to create businesses that not only fulfill market needs but also resonate with their communities. This spirit is evident in the diverse range of businesses being launched, from tech startups to artisanal goods, wellness services, and beyond.

While the entrepreneurial landscape offers opportunities, Black women face unique challenges that can hinder their success. Systemic barriers, including racial and gender bias, limit access to capital, mentorship, and networks that are crucial for business growth. Studies have shown that Black women receive significantly less funding than their white counterparts, which can stifle innovation and expansion.

Many Black women entrepreneurs juggle multiple roles—business owner, caregiver, community leader, and often, full-time employee. This balancing act can lead to burnout and stress, making it essential to develop effective time management strategies and prioritize self-care. The pressure to succeed while navigating these multiple responsibilities can be overwhelming, but many women find strength in their determination to create a better future for themselves and their families.

Implicit bias within the business world can manifest in various ways, from interactions with investors to customer perceptions. Black women often have to work harder to prove their competence and credibility, which can be both exhausting and demoralizing. Acknowledging and addressing these biases is vital for creating a more equitable entrepreneurial ecosystem.

A well-thought-out business plan is the foundation of any successful venture. For Black women entrepreneurs, this plan should not only outline financial projections and marketing strategies but also reflect their values, mission, and vision. It is essential to identify the unique selling propositions that differentiate their businesses in a competitive market. This clarity helps in attracting investors, partners, and customers who align with their vision.

Community plays a crucial role in the success of Black women entrepreneurs. Building a network of support—whether through other entrepreneurs, mentors, or local organizations—can provide invaluable resources and encouragement. Many Black women find strength in collaborating with one another, sharing insights, and pooling resources to overcome common challenges. This sense of community fosters resilience and creates a culture of collective upliftment.

Navigating the financial landscape is one of the most significant challenges for Black women entrepreneurs. Seeking out grants, crowdfunding opportunities, and alternative funding sources can provide crucial capital for business growth. Organizations dedicated to supporting minority-owned businesses, such as the Black Business Investment Fund and various local initiatives, can offer resources, mentorship, and funding opportunities tailored to the unique needs of Black women entrepreneurs.

In an increasingly digital world, leveraging technology is essential for business growth. Black women entrepreneurs are utilizing digital tools to enhance their operations, reach wider audiences, and streamline processes. From e-commerce platforms to social media marketing, technology can help level the playing field, allowing entrepreneurs to showcase their products and services on a global scale.

Establishing a strong online presence is vital for attracting and retaining customers. Black women entrepreneurs can utilize social media platforms to share their stories, connect with their audience, and promote their brands authentically. Creating engaging content that reflects their values and mission can foster a loyal customer base and increase visibility in a crowded market.

The rise of e-commerce has opened new avenues for Black women entrepreneurs to reach customers beyond their local markets. Setting up an online store allows for greater flexibility, enabling entrepreneurs to scale their businesses and adapt to changing consumer behaviors. The ability to analyze data and customer feedback also empowers women to make informed decisions about their products and services.

Effective leadership is a cornerstone of successful entrepreneurship. Black women must cultivate leadership skills that empower them to lead with confidence and clarity. This includes developing emotional intelligence, effective communication, and strategic thinking. Many entrepreneurs benefit from leadership training programs that focus on building these essential skills, enabling them to navigate challenges and inspire their teams.

Beyond profits, many Black women entrepreneurs are driven by a desire to create a positive impact in their communities. Developing a vision that encompasses social responsibility can guide decision-making and foster a sense of purpose. Whether through philanthropy, community engagement, or sustainable practices, aligning business goals with social impact can enhance brand loyalty and strengthen community ties.

As they achieve success, many Black women entrepreneurs feel a responsibility to mentor the next generation. Sharing experiences, insights, and resources not only empowers emerging entrepreneurs but also strengthens the community. Creating mentorship programs or engaging in local initiatives can foster a culture of support, ensuring that future generations of Black women entrepreneurs have the tools and networks they need to thrive.

Celebrating milestones, both big and small, is essential for maintaining motivation and momentum. Black women entrepreneurs should take the time to acknowledge their achievements, whether it's securing a major client, launching a new product, or reaching a revenue goal. These celebrations reinforce the hard work and dedication that goes into building a business and serve as inspiration for continued growth.

Storytelling is a powerful tool for Black women entrepreneurs. Sharing personal journeys and experiences can inspire others and foster a sense of connection within the community. By highlighting challenges and triumphs, entrepreneurs can create a narrative that resonates with others, encouraging aspiring business owners to pursue their dreams. Platforms such as podcasts, blogs, and social media are excellent avenues for sharing these stories.

Ultimately, running a business as a Black woman is about more than individual success; it's about building a legacy. Many entrepreneurs aspire to create businesses that reflect their values and contribute positively to their communities. This legacy can inspire future generations, demonstrating the power of resilience, innovation, and community support.

Running a business as a Black woman is a profound journey filled with challenges, triumphs, and opportunities for impact. It embodies the spirit of resilience, innovation, and community upliftment. By navigating systemic barriers, leveraging resources, and cultivating leadership, Black women entrepreneurs are not only transforming their lives but also reshaping the entrepreneurial landscape.

As they forge their paths, these women inspire others to embrace their identities, pursue their passions, and create businesses that reflect their values. The journey may be fraught with obstacles, but the strength and determination of Black women entrepreneurs shine brightly, illuminating a path for future generations to follow. In this tapestry of entrepreneurship, every thread represents a story of courage, creativity, and the unwavering pursuit of dreams.

Chapter 8

The Language of Silence: Communicating with My Husband as a Black Woman

In the intricate dance of marriage, communication is often considered the lifeblood of a relationship. Yet, there are moments when silence speaks volumes. As a Black woman in a marriage, the experience of communicating with my husband in silence is rich with unspoken emotions, cultural nuances, and deep understanding. This chapter explores the profound connection that can exist in the spaces between words, highlighting how silence can serve as a powerful form of communication, reflection, and intimacy within our partnership.

Silence between partners can be a shared language, an understanding that transcends words. In our marriage, silence is often a space where we connect on a deeper level, allowing us to express feelings that may be difficult to articulate. It's a moment to pause, breathe, and simply be present with each other. This shared silence fosters a sense of safety and belonging, creating an intimate atmosphere where both of us can reflect on our thoughts and feelings without the pressure of verbal expression.

As a Black woman, my experiences and emotions are often shaped by my cultural identity. In many Black families, silence can carry significant meaning—whether it's a moment of contemplation, a response to societal pressures, or a way to process grief and joy. The cultural nuances of silence in our relationship reflect our shared understanding of the complexities we face as individuals and as a couple. This backdrop enriches our unspoken communication, allowing us to navigate the world together with a profound sense of empathy and connection.

In moments of silence, body language becomes a powerful tool for communication. A gentle touch, a knowing glance, or the simple act of sitting close together conveys emotions that words sometimes fail to capture. For example, when I feel overwhelmed or anxious, my husband instinctively knows to draw near, wrapping his arms around me. This physical connection communicates comfort, reassurance, and solidarity without the need for spoken words.

Silence can also serve as a canvas for emotional expression. During times of joy, we may sit together, basking in the warmth of shared happiness, exchanging smiles and laughter that need no verbal accompaniment. Conversely, in moments of sorrow or frustration, silence allows us to process our feelings. We may sit in companionable quiet, acknowledging the weight of the moment without rushing to fill it with words. This emotional resonance deepens our bond, allowing us to support one another through life's highs and lows.

In any marriage, conflicts are inevitable. However, the way we navigate those conflicts can be enhanced by our ability to communicate in silence. When tensions rise, taking a moment of silence can allow both of us to step back, gather our thoughts, and approach the situation with clarity. Instead of reacting impulsively, we can use silence as a time to reflect on our feelings and the underlying issues at play.

Sometimes, silence is about giving each other space. As a Black woman, I am often aware of the external pressures and societal expectations that weigh on us. In those moments, my husband may sense that I need time to recharge and process my thoughts. By allowing for silence, we create an environment where both of us can express our needs without feeling rushed or pressured. This understanding fosters mutual respect and strengthens our connection.

There is an intimacy in shared silence that can be incredibly profound. Whether we are enjoying a quiet evening at home, watching a movie, or simply sitting together on the porch, these moments of silence become sacred. They are opportunities for us to connect deeply, free from distractions and the noise of the outside world. In these moments, the love and trust we share are palpable, reminding us of the strength of our partnership.

In our marriage, we have created rituals that incorporate silence as a form of connection. For instance, we sometimes engage in quiet walks, allowing the beauty of nature to envelop us while we enjoy each other's company in peace. These rituals not only enhance our bond but also provide a space for reflection and mindfulness. They remind us of the importance of being present with each other, cultivating a deeper understanding of our shared journey.

Silence is also a powerful tool for self-discovery. In the quiet moments, I often find clarity about my own thoughts and feelings. As a Black woman, the intersectionality of my identity can sometimes create internal conflict. In silence, I can explore these complexities, reflecting on my experiences and how they shape my relationship. This self-awareness enhances my ability to communicate more effectively with my husband, as I can articulate my feelings and needs with greater clarity.

Silence encourages vulnerability in our relationship. When we embrace moments of quiet, we create a safe space for each other to express our deepest fears and desires. This vulnerability fosters trust and intimacy, allowing us to connect on a level that transcends the superficial. In those moments of silence, we can explore our hopes for the future, our dreams, and the challenges we face, knowing that we are in this together.

While silence can be powerful, it can also lead to misunderstandings if unspoken words remain unaddressed. It's essential to acknowledge that silence doesn't always mean agreement or understanding. As a Black woman, I am aware of the societal pressures that can silence voices, including my own. This awareness prompts me to ensure that our moments of silence are balanced with open communication, addressing any underlying issues that may need to be vocalized.

To maintain a healthy balance, we engage in intentional check-ins. These conversations allow us to express our feelings about our silent moments, ensuring that we are on the same page and that our needs are being met. This practice reinforces our commitment to open communication, even when we find comfort in silence. By discussing our experiences, we strengthen our bond and enhance our understanding of each other's perspectives.

Talking to my husband in silence as a Black woman is a profound aspect of our relationship, reflecting love, understanding, and shared experiences. It is a language that transcends words, allowing us to connect on a deeper level. Through silence, we navigate the complexities of our identities, support each other through challenges, and celebrate our joys.

In a world that often prioritizes noise and distraction, the power of silence serves as a reminder of the importance of being present with one another. It is in these quiet moments that we find solace, strength, and intimacy, creating a foundation for a resilient and loving partnership. As we continue our journey together, the unspoken bond we share will remain a testament to the beauty of our connection—a connection that thrives in the silence, nurtured by understanding, love, and the unique tapestry of our lives as a Black couple.

Chapter 9

Embracing Wellness: A Journey of Healing and Empowerment for Black Women

Health is a multifaceted concept, encompassing physical, mental, and emotional well-being. For Black women, the journey toward holistic health is often fraught with unique challenges and systemic barriers. In this chapter, we will explore the intersection of culture, identity, and health while providing strategies for self-care, resilience, and empowerment. By sharing stories of strength and offering practical advice, we aim to illuminate pathways toward a healthier, more fulfilling life.

To appreciate the health landscape for Black women, it's essential to recognize the historical and societal factors that shape their experiences. From the legacy of slavery and segregation to contemporary issues like racial discrimination and health disparities, these elements have profound implications for physical and mental health.

The medical history of Black women is riddled with exploitation and mistrust. The notorious experimentation on enslaved women, such as the gynecological surgeries performed on Anarcha, Betsey, and Lucy by J. Marion Sims, laid a foundation of skepticism toward the medical establishment. This legacy continues to echo in the present, where Black women often report feeling dismissed or misdiagnosed by healthcare providers.

Today, Black women face significant health disparities, including higher rates of hypertension, diabetes, and maternal mortality compared to their white counterparts. These disparities can be attributed to a combination of socioeconomic factors, access to healthcare, and systemic bias within medical practices. Understanding these challenges is the first step toward addressing them.

One of the most potent tools for health and healing is the power of community. For Black women, strong familial ties and community networks can provide immense support during difficult times. Cultivating these connections can be a vital part of a holistic health strategy.

Creating a supportive community can take many forms. Whether through family gatherings, social clubs, or online groups, finding a tribe that understands and uplifts one another is crucial. Consider joining local organizations focused on health, wellness, or social justice to connect with like-minded individuals. These networks can offer emotional support, share resources, and foster a sense of belonging.

Storytelling has long been a tradition in Black culture, serving as a means of preserving history and sharing wisdom. Engaging in storytelling, whether through journaling, spoken word, or communal gatherings, can be therapeutic. Sharing experiences can help process trauma, foster connections, and empower others.

Physical health is a critical component of overall wellness. For Black women, it's vital to adopt a proactive approach to health that includes regular check-ups, physical activity, and nutrition.

Regular health check-ups are essential for prevention and early intervention. Black women should be aware of the specific screenings recommended for their age group, including mammograms, Pap smears, and blood pressure checks. Building a relationship with a healthcare provider who respects and understands their unique health needs is crucial.

Food is a cornerstone of culture and health. Embracing a balanced diet that incorporates traditional foods can promote wellness. Consider exploring recipes that celebrate cultural heritage while focusing on nutrient-dense ingredients. Cooking together with family or friends can also enhance the experience, making meals a time for connection and joy.

Physical activity is vital for maintaining health, reducing stress, and improving mood. Black women should seek out forms of exercise that resonate with them, whether it's dance, yoga, or team sports. Engaging in physical activities within community settings can also foster social connections, making exercise feel less like a chore and more like a celebration.

Mental health is often stigmatized, particularly in marginalized communities. For Black women, acknowledging and addressing mental health is crucial for overall well-being.

Conversations about mental health need to be normalized within families and communities. Educating oneself and others about mental health issues can dispel myths and encourage more open discussions. Consider hosting workshops or informal gatherings focused on mental wellness to foster dialogue.

Seeking Professional Help

Finding a therapist who understands the unique experiences of Black women can be transformative. Therapy can provide a safe space to explore feelings, cope with trauma, and develop coping strategies. Many organizations offer culturally competent therapists, and online platforms can expand access to mental health resources.

Mindfulness and Self-Care

Incorporating mindfulness practices, such as meditation or deep breathing exercises, can help manage stress and anxiety. Self-care routines should be personalized, including activities that bring joy and relaxation, whether it's reading, gardening, or creating art. Prioritizing self-care is not selfish; it's a necessary act of love and preservation.

Navigating the Healthcare System

Understanding how to navigate the healthcare system effectively can empower Black women to advocate for their health needs.

Health Literacy

Improving health literacy is essential. This includes understanding medical terminology, being informed about health conditions, and knowing patient rights. Resources such as local health workshops, online courses, and community health fairs can provide valuable information.

Advocacy and Empowerment

Advocating for oneself in medical settings is crucial. Black women should feel empowered to ask questions, seek second opinions, and voice concerns. Creating a list of questions before appointments can help ensure that all health concerns are addressed. Additionally, bringing a trusted friend or family member to appointments can provide support and help articulate concerns.

Building Relationships with Providers

Establishing a good relationship with healthcare providers can significantly impact health outcomes. Seek out practitioners who listen and respect individual health decisions. Building rapport can create an environment where Black women feel comfortable discussing their health openly.

Embracing Cultural Heritage

Cultural identity plays a vital role in health and wellness. For Black women, embracing their heritage can foster pride and enhance well-being.

Celebrating Traditions

Engaging in cultural traditions, whether through food, music, or art, can provide a sense of belonging and joy.

Participating in community events that celebrate Black culture can strengthen ties and promote a positive self-image.

Intergenerational Wisdom

The wisdom of older generations is invaluable. Listening to the stories and experiences of mothers, grandmothers, and aunts can provide insights into health practices and resilience. This intergenerational exchange not only preserves cultural heritage but also reinforces the importance of health.

Conclusion: The Path Forward

The journey toward health and wellness for Black women is complex yet profoundly rewarding. By understanding the historical context, nurturing community connections, prioritizing physical and mental health, and embracing cultural heritage, Black women can empower themselves and each other.

Health is not merely the absence of illness; it is a dynamic state of well-being that encompasses body, mind, and spirit. As Black women navigate the challenges of health, let us celebrate their strength, resilience, and unwavering spirit. Together, we can build a future where health equity is a reality, and every Black woman can thrive.

In this chapter, we have explored the essential aspects of health for Black women, emphasizing the need for community, self-advocacy, and cultural pride. By prioritizing holistic well-being, Black women can embark on a transformative journey toward empowerment and health.

Chapter 10

Motherhood: A Unique Journey

Motherhood is a profound and transformative experience, marked by its own set of challenges and joys. For Black mothers, this journey is further enriched and complicated by cultural expectations, societal pressures, and personal aspirations. The intersection of these factors creates a unique narrative that shapes how Black mothers navigate their roles. In this chapter, we will explore the complexities of being a Black mother, the balancing act between cultural expectations and personal aspirations, and the support systems that can empower these remarkable women in their journeys.

The Landscape of Black Motherhood

Black motherhood exists within a rich tapestry of history, culture, and resilience. The legacy of Black women as mothers stretches back to the times of enslavement, where they were often forced to navigate the harsh realities of oppression while nurturing and protecting their families. This historical context continues to influence the modern experience of Black motherhood, as women today grapple with the weight of expectations from their families, communities, and society at large.

Historical Context and Its Impact

Understanding the historical context of Black motherhood helps illuminate the current challenges faced by Black mothers. From the era of slavery, where Black women often had to care for the children of their enslavers while being separated from their own, to the civil rights movement, where mothers fought for their children's rights and dignity, the narrative of Black motherhood is steeped in resilience.

Today, Black mothers continue to face systemic barriers, including racial discrimination, economic disparities, and social stigmas. These challenges can manifest in various ways, from struggles in accessing quality healthcare and education to the daily stressors of navigating a world that often devalues their contributions.

The Joys of Motherhood

Despite the challenges, motherhood brings immense joy and fulfillment. The bond between a mother and her child is profound, often characterized by unconditional love, shared experiences, and deep emotional connections. For many Black mothers, these moments of joy provide a counterbalance to the struggles they face.

Celebrating Cultural Heritage

One of the joys of being a Black mother is the ability to pass down cultural heritage and traditions. Many Black mothers take great pride in educating their children about their history, culture, and the contributions of their ancestors. Whether through storytelling, music, art, or culinary traditions, these experiences help children develop a strong sense of identity and belonging.

Celebrating cultural heritage can also involve rituals and practices that strengthen familial bonds. From family gatherings centered around food to community events that honor cultural milestones, these traditions create a sense of continuity and connection. They remind Black mothers of the strength found in community and heritage, even amidst challenges.

Balancing Cultural Expectations with Personal Aspirations

Navigating the expectations of family and community while pursuing personal aspirations can be particularly challenging for Black mothers. Cultural norms often dictate how motherhood should be experienced, leading to pressure to conform to specific ideals. This section will explore how Black mothers can balance these expectations with their own dreams and ambitions.

The Weight of Expectations

Cultural expectations surrounding motherhood can be both uplifting and burdensome. Many Black mothers feel a strong obligation to uphold family values, support their children, and contribute to their communities. While these expectations can foster a sense of purpose, they can also lead to feelings of guilt and inadequacy when personal aspirations take a backseat.

For instance, a mother may feel torn between pursuing a career and being present for her children, especially in cultures that place a high value on maternal involvement. This internal conflict can be amplified by societal narratives that often portray Black mothers in stereotypical roles, neglecting the multifaceted realities of their lives.

Redefining Success

In order to navigate these pressures, many Black mothers are redefining what success looks like for them. This process involves acknowledging personal aspirations and finding ways to integrate them into their roles as mothers. It means understanding that being a good mother does not necessitate sacrificing one's dreams; instead, it can involve modeling resilience, ambition, and self-care for their children.

For instance, a mother pursuing higher education might involve her children in her journey, sharing her experiences and demonstrating the importance of lifelong learning. This not only enriches her own life but also teaches her children valuable lessons about perseverance and the pursuit of dreams.

The Role of Support Systems

Support systems are vital for Black mothers as they navigate the complexities of motherhood. These systems can provide emotional, social, and practical support, helping to alleviate some of the pressures faced. This section explores the various forms of support that can empower Black mothers.

Family Support

Family, often seen as the first line of support, plays a crucial role in the lives of Black mothers. Extended family members, such as grandparents, aunts, and cousins, often step in to provide assistance with childcare, emotional support, and shared responsibilities. This network can create a sense of community that helps alleviate the pressures of motherhood.

However, it's essential for mothers to communicate their needs and establish boundaries. While family support is invaluable, it's also crucial to maintain a balance that respects personal space and autonomy. Open conversations about expectations and roles can lead to healthier family dynamics, allowing for a more supportive environment.

Friendships and Community

Friendships can also serve as vital sources of support. Many Black mothers find solace in connecting with other mothers who share similar experiences. These friendships provide a safe space for sharing challenges, celebrating successes, and seeking advice.

Participating in community organizations focused on supporting Black families can further strengthen these connections. Whether through parenting groups, cultural organizations, or local initiatives, these spaces foster camaraderie and shared understanding. They remind mothers that they are not alone in their journeys and that community support is essential.

Mental Health and Self-Care

The mental health of Black mothers is a critical aspect of their overall well-being. The pressures of motherhood, combined with societal stressors, can lead to feelings of isolation, anxiety, and burnout. Prioritizing mental health and self-care is essential for navigating the demands of motherhood.

Breaking the Stigma

Historically, discussions about mental health within the Black community have been stigmatized. Many Black mothers may feel hesitant to seek help due to fears of being misunderstood or judged. However, breaking this stigma is crucial for fostering a culture of openness and support.

Engaging with mental health professionals who understand the unique challenges faced by Black mothers can be transformative. Therapy can provide a safe space for processing emotions, developing coping strategies, and finding balance amidst the chaos of motherhood. Additionally, community-based mental health resources can offer culturally relevant support.

Prioritizing Self-Care

Self-care is not a luxury; it's a necessity for Black mothers. Finding time to engage in activities that recharge the spirit—whether through exercise, hobbies, or simply resting—can have a profound impact on overall well-being. Encouraging self-care practices within the family can also be a powerful lesson for children, teaching them the importance of nurturing their own well-being.

Creating routines that prioritize self-care can help mothers manage stress and maintain a sense of identity outside of motherhood. This could involve setting aside time each week for personal interests, establishing boundaries around work and family time, or even engaging in mindfulness practices.

The Intersection of Identity

The journey of Black motherhood is further complicated by the intersectionality of identities. Issues of race, class, and gender all play a role in shaping the experiences of Black mothers. Navigating these intersections requires awareness and resilience, as mothers advocate for themselves and their children.

Advocating for Children

One of the most profound responsibilities of motherhood is advocating for children. Black mothers often find themselves in positions where they must fight for their children's rights and opportunities, whether in education, healthcare, or the legal system. Understanding systemic inequalities and being equipped to navigate them is crucial for ensuring that their children receive the support they need.

This advocacy can take many forms, from actively engaging in school boards to participating in community activism. By modeling advocacy, Black mothers teach their children the importance of standing up for themselves and their communities, empowering the next generation.

Celebrating Milestones and Achievements

Celebrating milestones is an essential part of the motherhood journey. From birthdays to graduations, these moments serve as reminders of growth and resilience. For Black mothers, these celebrations can also be opportunities to honor cultural heritage and family traditions.

Creating Lasting Memories

Black mothers often find joy in creating lasting memories with their children. Whether through elaborate birthday parties that reflect cultural themes or family gatherings that celebrate achievements, these moments become cherished parts of the family narrative. They reinforce the importance of family bonds and cultural identity.

Documenting these milestones through photos, videos, or journals can help create a legacy for future generations. Sharing stories of resilience, love, and celebration fosters a sense of belonging and continuity within the family.

Conclusion: Embracing the Journey

Motherhood is a unique journey for Black women, marked by its challenges and joys. The complexities of balancing cultural expectations with personal aspirations require resilience, advocacy, and a strong support system. By embracing their identities, breaking down stigmas, and prioritizing self-care, Black mothers can navigate this journey with strength and grace.

Ultimately, the story of Black motherhood is one of empowerment and legacy. Each mother contributes to a rich tapestry of experiences, shaping the lives of her children and creating a brighter future. As we celebrate the unique journey of Black motherhood, let us continue to support one another, uplift our communities, and honor the profound impact of motherhood in all its forms. Through love, resilience, and solidarity, we can navigate the complexities of this journey together.

Chapter 11

Finding Your Tribe: The Power of Community for Black Women

In a world that often feels overwhelming, the question of whom to ask for help can be a daunting one, especially for Black women. Balancing numerous roles whether as professionals, caregivers, or community leaders can create a unique set of challenges. Yet, within these challenges lies the profound strength of community. This chapter explores the different avenues for seeking help, the importance of building a supportive network, and the transformative power of solidarity among Black women.

To navigate life's complexities, understanding the landscape of support available is crucial. For Black women, this landscape is often shaped by cultural, social, and historical contexts. The legacy of resilience runs deep; our ancestors faced adversities that demanded strength and solidarity. Today, this legacy manifests in various forms of support systems family, friends, mentors, and community organizations.

1. Family: The First Line of Defense

Traditionally, family is the first place many turn to for help. In many Black families, the concept of kinship extends beyond blood relations. This broad definition can include close friends and community members who feel like family. These relationships create a foundation of trust and understanding, offering a safe space to express vulnerabilities without fear of judgment.

When seeking help from family, it's essential to communicate openly about your needs. Whether it's emotional support during a tough period or practical help like childcare, articulating your needs can foster deeper connections. Remember, it's okay to lean on your family—not just for big crises but also for everyday challenges.

2. Friends: Your Chosen Family

Friendships can be a lifeline. For many Black women, friends become a chosen family, providing camaraderie and understanding that can sometimes feel lacking in other areas of life. These friendships often act as a mirror reflecting shared experiences, cultural backgrounds, and mutual support.

When reaching out to friends for help, it's important to be vulnerable. Share your struggles, both big and small. This openness can invite deeper conversations, allowing your friends to offer support that resonates with your specific needs. Additionally, fostering a reciprocal relationship where you also support your friends can strengthen these bonds, creating a robust network of mutual aid.

3. Mentors and Professional Networks

In the professional realm, mentorship can be invaluable. Finding a mentor—someone who understands the unique challenges faced by Black women in the workplace—can provide guidance, encouragement, and a wealth of knowledge. Mentors can help navigate career paths, advocate for opportunities, and offer insights into overcoming systemic barriers.

To find a mentor, consider reaching out to individuals within your network or professional organizations that support Black women. Initiate conversations about your goals and seek advice on specific challenges. Many professionals are eager to give back, and your initiative may inspire them to invest in your growth.

4. Community Organizations and Support Groups

Community organizations play a significant role in providing resources and support. Numerous organizations focus on the empowerment of Black women, offering workshops, networking events, and mental health resources. Engaging with these organizations can help you connect with others who share similar struggles and aspirations.

Support groups can also provide a space for healing and sharing experiences. Whether focused on mental health, parenting, or professional development, these groups foster a sense of belonging. They remind you that you are not alone in your challenges and that collective experiences can lead to collective healing.

Asking for help often requires vulnerability. For many Black women, societal expectations can make this difficult. The stereotype of the "strong Black woman" can create pressure to appear resilient and self-sufficient at all times.

However, embracing vulnerability is a powerful act of courage.

When you allow yourself to be vulnerable, you open the door for others to do the same. This shared vulnerability can deepen connections and create a supportive environment where everyone feels safe to express their needs. Remember, asking for help is not a sign of weakness; it's an acknowledgment of your humanity.

Creating a robust support network takes time and intention. Here are some steps to help you build and nurture your community:

1. Define Your Needs

Take time to reflect on what kind of help you need. Are you looking for emotional support, professional guidance, or practical assistance? Defining your needs will help you identify who in your network can provide that support.

2. Reach Out

Don't hesitate to reach out to those who can help. Whether it's a family member, friend, mentor, or community leader, initiating the conversation Is key. Be clear about what you're looking for and why you think they can help.

3. Offer Help in Return

Support is a two-way street. When you seek help, also be prepared to offer your support to others. This reciprocity strengthens relationships and fosters a sense of community.

4. Join Groups and Organizations

Engage with local organizations that empower Black women. Participate in workshops, networking events, and community activities. This involvement can help you meet like-minded individuals who can become part of your support network.

5. Prioritize Self-Care

Taking care of yourself is vital in maintaining your capacity to support others and accept help when needed. Prioritize self-care practices that recharge your spirit, whether through meditation, exercise, or creative outlets.

In today's digital age, online communities have become a powerful resource for connection and support. Social media platforms and online forums dedicated to Black women can provide a sense of belonging and a wealth of resources. These spaces allow for sharing experiences, seeking advice, and celebrating achievements.

However, it's essential to navigate these spaces thoughtfully. Engage with communities that align with your values and offer positive support. Be mindful of the impact of negative interactions and prioritize your well-being in these digital environments.

As Black women, our collective strength is a force to be reckoned with. Celebrating each other's achievements and acknowledging the challenges we face can foster a sense of unity and empowerment. When we lift each other up, we create a ripple effect that extends beyond our individual lives.

Engage in practices that celebrate this strength. Whether through storytelling, community events, or mentorship programs, highlighting the contributions of Black women can inspire others and reinforce the importance of solidarity.

Asking for help is a journey, one that requires courage and intention. For Black women, this journey is intertwined with cultural narratives of resilience and community. By embracing vulnerability, building supportive networks, and seeking help from various sources, we can navigate life's challenges together.

In a world that often seeks to divide, let us remember the strength found in community. By lifting each other up and creating spaces for open dialogue, we can empower ourselves and future generations of Black women. Together, we can transform the act of asking for help from a daunting challenge into a powerful testament to our collective strength and resilience.

In this journey, remember: you are not alone. Your tribe is out there, waiting to support and uplift you. Seek them out, embrace your vulnerability, and celebrate the incredible power of community.

Chapter 12

Loving a Lost Son: A Journey of Grief and Resilience

The bond between a mother and her child is profound, often described as the purest form of love. For Black women, this bond carries a unique weight, particularly when faced with the loss of a son. The journey of loving a lost son is filled with deep grief, complex emotions, and an unyielding resilience that shapes a mother's identity. This chapter delves into the heart-wrenching experience of losing a son, the nuances of grief, the societal implications of such loss, and the eventual path toward healing and remembrance.

Losing a child is a tragedy no parent should endure, but for many Black mothers, this heartbreak can be magnified by societal factors. The statistics are stark: Black boys are disproportionately affected by violence, systemic racism, and a host of societal inequities. The loss of a son can feel like a double tragedy—a personal loss intertwined with the weight of cultural and systemic injustices.

The moment of loss is often surreal. It can feel as if time stands still, the world around you blurring into the background as the reality of the situation sinks in. For many mothers, the news of their son's death—whether through violence, illness, or accident—comes like a thunderclap, shattering their world and leaving an indelible mark on their hearts.

In the immediate aftermath, the experience can be overwhelming. Waves of shock, disbelief, and anger can wash over a mother, each emotion more intense than the last. The finality of death brings with it an acute sense of helplessness, as well as a torrent of questions: Why did this happen? What could I have done differently? How will I ever move forward?

Grief is a deeply personal journey, and it manifests differently for everyone. For Black mothers, the societal context can complicate this process. The expectations to remain strong, to uphold the image of the "strong Black woman," can create an internal struggle.

Within the Black community, there exists an unspoken expectation for mothers to embody resilience in the face of adversity. This stereotype—often rooted in historical contexts where Black women have had to endure immense suffering—can add layers of pressure to grieve in silence, to bear the pain without showing vulnerability.

Yet, grief is not a linear process; it does not adhere to societal expectations or timelines. For many mothers, this complexity can lead to feelings of isolation. The fear of being seen as weak or overly emotional can prevent them from seeking support or expressing their pain openly. It becomes vital to understand that vulnerability is not a weakness but a necessary part of healing.

The emotions that accompany grief can be multifaceted and can shift unexpectedly. A mother may experience profound sadness, anger, guilt, and even moments of joy when remembering her son. These conflicting emotions can be disorienting, making it challenging to find a sense of normalcy.

Sadness: This is perhaps the most palpable emotion. It can manifest as a deep ache in the heart, a longing for the presence of the lost child. It can be triggered by memories, moments of silence, or even the laughter of other children, reminding the mother of what she has lost.

Anger: Anger can arise from various sources: anger at the circumstances of the loss, anger at the world for being unfair, anger directed at the deceased for leaving. This anger is a valid response, a way of processing the overwhelming sense of injustice that often accompanies the loss of a child.

Guilt: Many mothers grapple with guilt, questioning their actions or inactions. Did I do enough? Could I have protected him? This guilt can linger, complicating the grieving process.

Joyful Memories: Amidst the sorrow, there can be moments of joy when recalling happy times spent together. These memories can serve as both a balm and a source of pain, reminding the mother of the love that once filled her life.

The Role of Community

In the wake of such a profound loss, community can play a crucial role in the healing process. For Black mothers, the support of family, friends, and community members can provide a lifeline. However, navigating this support can also be complex.

Seeking Support

When a son is lost, the instinct to seek comfort often leads to the embrace of a close-knit community. Family members, friends, and even neighbors can offer solace, providing a space to share memories and reflect on the impact of the loss. However, the challenge lies in finding the right balance between seeking support and feeling overwhelmed by the attention that such a tragedy attracts.

It's essential for mothers to articulate their needs during this time. Some may find comfort in talking about their son, while others may prefer silence and reflection. Being vocal about these preferences can help guide friends and family in offering the right kind of support.

The Power of Collective Grief

In many Black communities, collective grief is a powerful force. Funerals and memorial services become communal experiences, where friends and family gather to honor the lost child and support the grieving mother. These gatherings can serve as a reminder of the strength found in unity, transforming individual sorrow into a shared experience.

During these moments, storytelling often takes center stage. Friends and family share anecdotes and memories, painting a vivid picture of the life that was lost. This act of remembrance can be cathartic, allowing the mother to feel connected to her son in a new way even as she mourns his absence.

Navigating the Legal and Social Realities

For many Black mothers, the loss of a son can also involve navigating complicated legal and social realities. Whether the death was the result of violence, systemic injustice, or other societal issues, these factors can add layers of complexity to the grieving process.

The Impact of Violence

In cases where violence is involved—be it police violence, gang-related incidents, or community violence—the mother often finds herself thrust into a public narrative. This can involve dealing with law enforcement, media scrutiny, and community advocacy. The pressure to become an advocate for change can be immense, as the mother may feel compelled to speak out against the injustices that led to her son's death.

This advocacy can be a double-edged sword. On one hand, it provides a sense of purpose and a way to honor her son's memory. On the other, it can also reopen wounds, bringing the pain of loss to the forefront as she navigates public discourse about her child's life and death.

Seeking Justice

The quest for justice can be a long and arduous journey. Many mothers find themselves entangled in legal battles, seeking accountability for their son's death. This process can be emotionally draining, often exacerbating feelings of grief and frustration. For some, the journey becomes a testament to their love for their lost son—a way to ensure that his life had meaning and that his story would not be forgotten.

The Path to Healing

While the journey of grief can be long and winding, healing is possible. For Black mothers, this journey often involves embracing their emotions, seeking support, and finding ways to honor their son's memory.

Embracing Emotions

Allowing oneself to fully experience the pain of loss is a crucial step toward healing. This may mean crying, expressing anger, or even seeking professional help. Therapy can provide a safe space for mothers to process their feelings, explore their grief, and work through the complexities of their emotions.

Finding ways to honor the memory of a lost son can be an essential part of the healing journey. This could involve creating a memorial, participating in community events, or even establishing a scholarship in his name. These acts of remembrance not only keep the memory of the child alive but also provide a sense of purpose in the aftermath of loss.

Creating Rituals: Many mothers find solace in creating rituals that commemorate their son. This could be as simple as lighting a candle on significant dates or as elaborate as organizing an annual gathering to celebrate his life. These rituals can serve as a way to connect with the lost child and create a lasting legacy.

Sharing Stories: Telling stories about the son can be therapeutic. This might involve writing about him, sharing memories with friends, or even engaging in community storytelling events. Sharing his life with others keeps his spirit alive and reminds the mother that her son was loved and cherished.

Despite the profound pain of losing a son, the love a mother holds for her child remains unbreakable. This love can be a source of strength, guiding her through the darkest moments of grief.

For many mothers, the love they have for their lost sons transforms into a driving force for change. This might manifest as activism, community service, or advocacy work aimed at addressing the systemic issues that contribute to violence against Black boys. Channeling grief into action not only honors the memory of the child but also creates a legacy that can impact future generations.

Resilience is a hallmark of the Black experience, deeply rooted in history and culture. Black mothers, drawing from this legacy, often find ways to rise from their grief, transforming their pain into a powerful narrative of strength. This resilience is not about forgetting the loss but rather about integrating it into their lives in a way that honors their son while allowing them to move forward.

Loving a lost son as a Black woman is a journey filled with heartache, complexity, and ultimately, resilience. The weight of grief is heavy, but so too is the love that endures beyond death. Through community support, personal reflection, and acts of remembrance, Black mothers can navigate this profound loss, finding ways to honor their sons while also embracing their own paths toward healing.

As these mothers continue their journeys, they carry with them the legacy of their lost sons—a legacy marked by love, resilience, and the unbreakable bond between mother and child. Though the pain may never fully dissipate, the love remains a guiding light, illuminating the path forward as they seek to create a world where their sons' lives—and the lives of all children—are valued and protected. In this journey, they remind us all of the power of love to transcend even the deepest of sorrows.

Chapter 13

Navigating Health Disparities

Health disparities are significant differences in health outcomes and access to healthcare services that are often influenced by socio-economic status, geography, ethnicity, and gender. Among these disparities, the health issues affecting Black women are particularly alarming. This chapter delves into the systemic health issues impacting Black women, the importance of self-advocacy in healthcare, and strategies to navigate these challenges effectively.

Health disparities refer to the differences in health status or healthcare access between different population groups. These disparities are often rooted in social, economic, and environmental disadvantages. Black women, in particular, face a unique set of challenges that contribute to poorer health outcomes compared to their white counterparts and even Black men. Factors contributing to these disparities include:

Socioeconomic Status: Many Black women are disproportionately affected by poverty, which limits access to quality healthcare, nutritious food, and safe living conditions. Economic instability can lead to stress and a higher prevalence of chronic diseases.

Access to Healthcare: Black women often experience barriers to accessing healthcare services, including lack of health insurance, transportation issues, and inadequate availability of culturally competent providers. These barriers can result in delayed diagnoses and treatment.

Racism and Discrimination: Systemic racism in healthcare can manifest as biased treatment by healthcare providers, leading to misdiagnosis, undertreatment, or overtreatment of conditions. This discrimination can discourage Black women from seeking care altogether.

Cultural Factors: Cultural perceptions of health and wellness can influence how Black women approach healthcare. Historical mistrust in the medical system, stemming from unethical practices like the Tuskegee Study, can lead to hesitancy in seeking medical help.

Chronic Stress: The cumulative effects of racism, discrimination, and socio-economic challenges contribute to chronic stress, which is linked to a variety of health issues, including hypertension, diabetes, and mental health disorders.

Understanding the specific health issues that disproportionately affect Black women is crucial for addressing health disparities:

Maternal Health

Black women experience significantly higher rates of maternal mortality compared to white women. Factors contributing to this disparity include:

Access to Prenatal Care: Limited access to quality prenatal care can lead to complications during pregnancy and childbirth. Black women often encounter systemic barriers that hinder timely access to necessary medical services.

Preexisting Conditions: Conditions such as hypertension and diabetes, which are more prevalent among Black women, can complicate pregnancies and increase the risk of maternal mortality.

Racism in Healthcare: Studies have shown that Black women are often not taken seriously by healthcare providers when reporting pain or complications during pregnancy, leading to inadequate care.

Chronic Diseases

Black women are at a higher risk for several chronic diseases, including:

Heart Disease: This is the leading cause of death among women in the United States, with Black women facing higher rates of hypertension and other cardiovascular issues.

Diabetes: The prevalence of diabetes is significantly higher among Black women, often linked to lifestyle factors and limited access to preventive healthcare.

Obesity: Black women have higher obesity rates, influenced by a combination of economic factors, food deserts, and cultural attitudes toward body image and health.

Mental Health

Mental health issues are often stigmatized, particularly within the Black community. Black women may face:

Higher Stress Levels: The intersection of race and gender can lead to unique stressors, including the pressure to succeed in professional environments and navigate societal expectations.

Underdiagnosis and Misdiagnosis: Mental health conditions may be overlooked or misdiagnosed in Black women due to biases in the healthcare system.

Access to Mental Health Services: Barriers such as cost, stigma, and lack of culturally competent providers can prevent Black women from seeking necessary mental health care.

Reproductive Health

Reproductive health issues, including access to contraception and family planning services, are critical for Black women. Disparities in reproductive health can lead to unintended pregnancies and limited control over reproductive choices.

Self-advocacy is a vital skill for navigating the complexities of the healthcare system. For Black women, cultivating self-advocacy can lead to better health outcomes and empower them to take control of their health. Here are several reasons why self-advocacy is particularly important:

Empowerment

Self-advocacy empowers Black women to voice their health concerns, ask questions, and demand appropriate care. This empowerment can lead to better communication with healthcare providers, ensuring that their needs and preferences are understood and respected.

Increased Knowledge

Educating oneself about health conditions, treatment options, and healthcare rights is essential for effective self-advocacy. Knowledge can help Black women navigate the healthcare system more confidently and make informed decisions about their health.

Building Relationships

Establishing a trusting relationship with healthcare providers is crucial. Self-advocacy encourages Black women to seek out providers who are culturally competent and respectful, fostering a collaborative approach to healthcare.

Reducing Mistrust

By actively participating in their healthcare processes, Black women can reduce feelings of mistrust toward the medical system. Engaging in open dialogue with providers and seeking transparency can help bridge the gap created by historical injustices.

Navigating the healthcare system can be daunting, but there are several strategies Black women can employ to advocate for their health effectively:

Prepare for Appointments

Preparation is key to effective self-advocacy. Before a healthcare visit, Black women should:

Make a List of Questions: Write down any concerns or questions about symptoms, medications, or treatment options to ensure they are addressed during the appointment.

Keep a Health Journal: Documenting health symptoms, medications, and lifestyle factors can provide valuable information to healthcare providers.

Research Conditions: Understanding potential health conditions and treatment options can enhance discussions with providers and facilitate informed decision-making.

Seek Support

Having a support system can enhance self-advocacy efforts:

Bring a Friend or Family Member: Accompanying someone to medical appointments can provide emotional support and help communicate concerns.

Join Support Groups: Engaging with others who share similar experiences can provide valuable insights and encouragement.

Communicate Effectively

Effective communication is essential for advocating for one's health:

Be Honest About Symptoms: Clearly articulating symptoms and concerns can help providers make accurate diagnoses and treatment plans.

Request Clarification: If something is unclear, it is vital to ask providers to explain terms or procedures in simpler language.

Express Preferences: Black women should feel empowered to discuss their preferences regarding treatment options and care.

Know Your Rights

Understanding healthcare rights is crucial for self-advocacy:

Familiarize with Patient Rights: Knowing rights as a patient can help Black women advocate for themselves and hold providers accountable.

Report Discrimination: If encountering discrimination or bias, it is important to report these incidents to the appropriate authorities or organizations.

Community-Based Approaches to Address Health Disparities

While individual self-advocacy is vital, community-based approaches are equally important for addressing systemic health disparities affecting Black women. These approaches can include:

Health Education and Outreach

Community organizations can play a significant role in educating Black women about health issues, preventive care, and available resources. Outreach programs can help bridge gaps in knowledge and access to care.

Culturally Competent Care

Promoting culturally competent care within healthcare systems is essential. Training healthcare providers to understand the unique experiences of Black women can improve patient-provider relationships and health outcomes.

Policy Advocacy

Advocating for policy changes at local, state, and national levels can help address systemic issues affecting Black women's health. This can include pushing for expanded access to healthcare, funding for community health programs, and initiatives aimed at reducing health disparities.

Research and Data Collection

Investing in research focused on the health issues disproportionately affecting Black women is crucial. Collecting disaggregated data can help identify specific needs and inform targeted interventions.

Navigating health disparities is a multifaceted challenge, particularly for Black women who face unique systemic barriers. Understanding these disparities and the importance of self-advocacy can empower Black women to take control of their health. By fostering a culture of self-advocacy and supporting community-based initiatives, we can work towards reducing health disparities and improving health outcomes for Black women. The journey towards health equity requires collective action, informed advocacy, and a commitment to dismantling the systemic barriers that perpetuate disparities in health and healthcare.

The Bio of Chiquita D. Felder-Stephenson

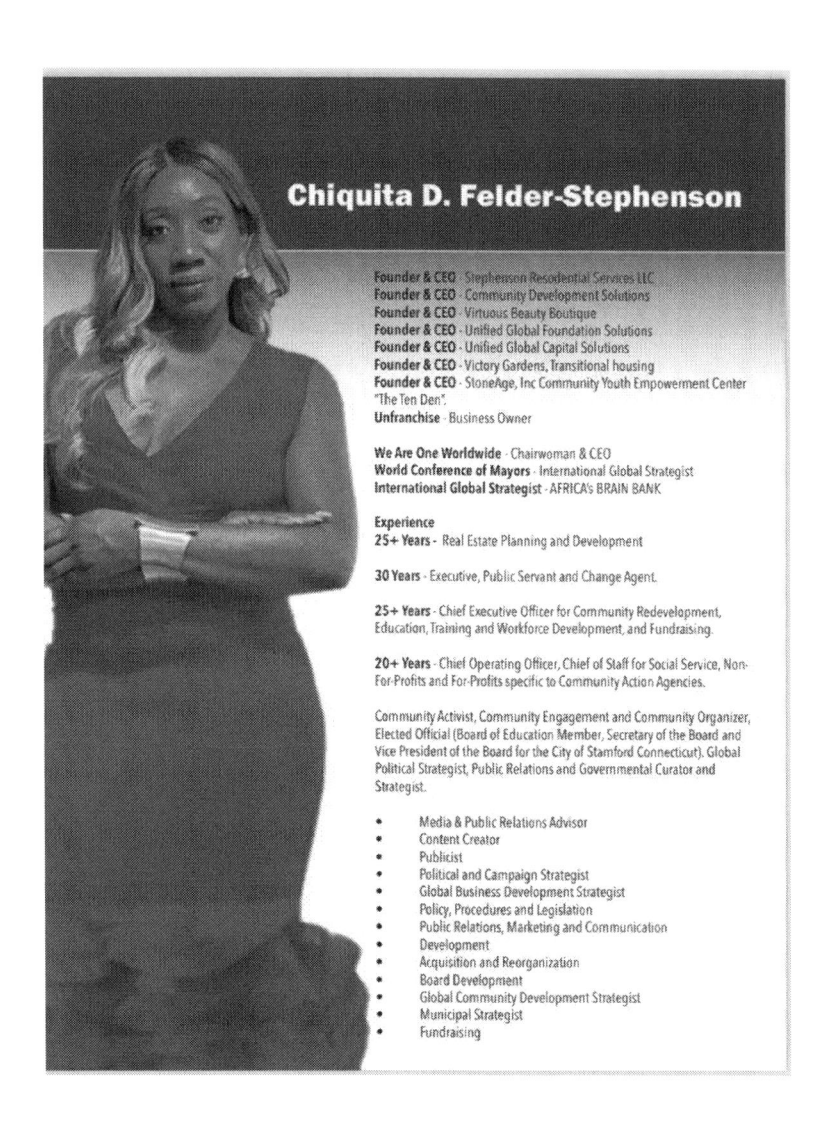

Chiquita D. Felder-Stephenson

Founder & CEO - Stephenson Residential Services LLC
Founder & CEO - Community Development Solutions
Founder & CEO - Virtuous Beauty Boutique
Founder & CEO - Unified Global Foundation Solutions
Founder & CEO - Unified Global Capital Solutions
Founder & CEO - Victory Gardens, Transitional housing
Founder & CEO - StoneAge, Inc Community Youth Empowerment Center "The Ten Den".
Unfranchise - Business Owner

We Are One Worldwide - Chairwoman & CEO
World Conference of Mayors - International Global Strategist
International Global Strategist - AFRICA'S BRAIN BANK

Experience
25+ Years - Real Estate Planning and Development

30 Years - Executive, Public Servant and Change Agent.

25+ Years - Chief Executive Officer for Community Redevelopment, Education, Training and Workforce Development, and Fundraising.

20+ Years - Chief Operating Officer, Chief of Staff for Social Service, Non-For-Profits and For-Profits specific to Community Action Agencies.

Community Activist, Community Engagement and Community Organizer, Elected Official (Board of Education Member, Secretary of the Board and Vice President of the Board for the City of Stamford Connecticut). Global Political Strategist, Public Relations and Governmental Curator and Strategist.

- Media & Public Relations Advisor
- Content Creator
- Publicist
- Political and Campaign Strategist
- Global Business Development Strategist
- Policy, Procedures and Legislation
- Public Relations, Marketing and Communication
- Development
- Acquisition and Reorganization
- Board Development
- Global Community Development Strategist
- Municipal Strategist
- Fundraising